TUDOR
1485–1603

STUART
1603–17

VICTORIAN
1837–1901

MODERN TIMES
1901–NOW

children's HISTORY of DERBYSHIRE

Written by
Pauline Chandler

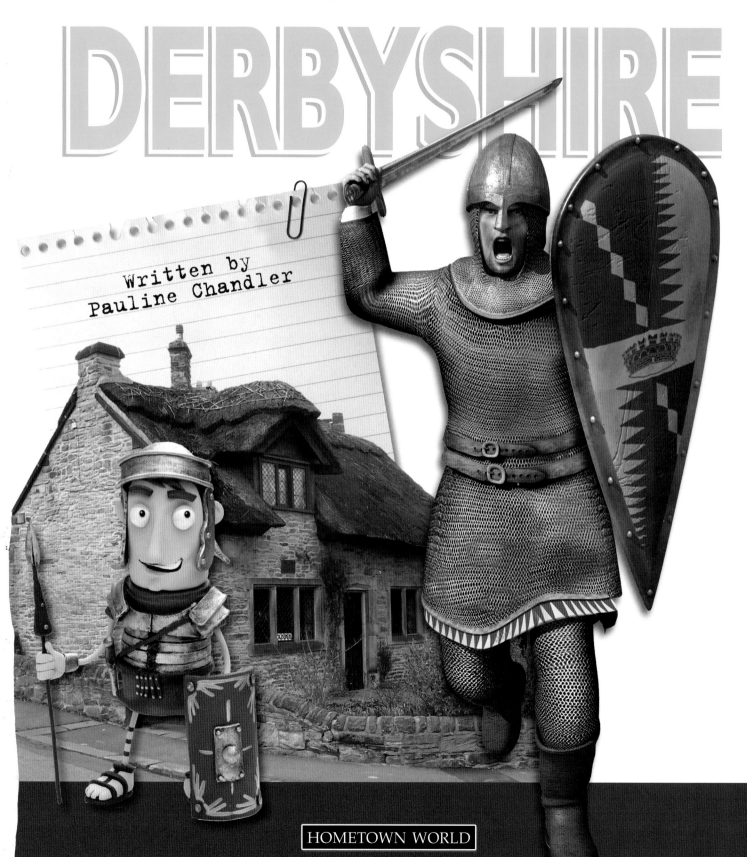

HOMETOWN WORLD

How well do you know Derbyshire?

Have you ever wondered what it would have been like living in Derbyshire when the Vikings arrived? What about going to visit Matlock Bath on a brand new steam locomotive? This book will uncover the important and exciting things that happened in this wonderful county.

Some rather brainy folk have worked on this book to make sure it's fun and informative. So what are you waiting for? Peel back the pages and be amazed at Derbyshire's very own story.

'Spot this!' game with hints on something to find in the county

THE FACTS

Intriguing photos

Fun Facts to amaze you!

THE EVIDENCE

Timeline shows which period (dates and people) each spread is talking about

Imaginary account of what it was like for children growing up in Derbyshire

Summary explaining how we know about the past

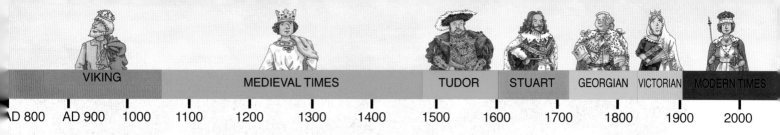

Contents

Derventio

Marcus and Cornelius are returning to the fort in Derventio after a hard day's work. They have been busy repairing roads in the heavy rain and feel cold, wet and tired. They don't think much of this British weather and are looking forward to visiting the baths before dinner.

As the soldiers enter the fort, a familiar aroma wafts past Marcus's nose. "Smells like my favourite for dinner tonight," he says. "Stuffed dormice – delicious!"

Roman Invasion

In AD 43 the Romans invaded Britain and conquered the local Celtic tribes. In Derbyshire, the two main Celtic tribes were the Brigantes and the Corieltauvi. Soon after the Romans arrived, they built forts at Buxton, Chesterfield, Derby, Brough and Glossop, among others. In Derby, the Romans named their fort Derventio, after the River Derwent.

By AD 90 there was a busy town or 'vicus' attached to the fort at Derventio, where Romans and Celts lived and traded. Pottery was made there, including the new Roman mortars, or shallow dishes, for pounding herbs and spices. The Romans mined lead and made peace through trade. Within a few years the native people and the Romans were friends and neighbours.

These pad stones in Marcus Street, Derby, were once the bases of an entrance to a Roman building.

4

AD **43** ROMANS INVADE...AROUND AD **80** ROMANS BUILD FORT AT DERVENTIO...

Roman Roads

Because of its position in the Midlands, Derbyshire was an important crossroads for the Romans, with direct routes to the rest of the country. One of the major roads was Rykneld Street, running from modern-day Gloucestershire, through Derbyshire to South Yorkshire. Parts of the road can still be seen in Denby. In some places, modern roads lie over the top of the old Roman road, such as Long Lane, west of Derby.

SPOT THIS!

This street sign in the Little Chester area of Derby recalls the city's Roman past. Can you spot it?

CÆSAR

A typical Roman fort

ouch!

FUN FACT
Roman soldiers rubbed their arms and legs with stinging nettles to warm them against the cold, wet British weather.

Changes

The Romans brought a new way of life. Their stone-built villas were more comfortable than the Britons' wooden huts, with underfloor heating and open roofed verandas. They made fine glass and pottery, new foods and tools. They gave us reading and writing, Latin, new gods and goddesses and better hygiene with their bathhouses.

Derwent comes from the Celtic word 'dyr', which means oak tree, and 'venta', meaning market.

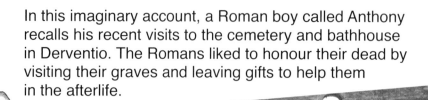

CELT
500 BC

ROMAN
AD 43–410

ANGLO-SAXON
AD 450–1066

VIKING
AD 865–1066

MEDIEVA
TIMES
1066–148

In this imaginary account, a Roman boy called Anthony recalls his recent visits to the cemetery and bathhouse in Derventio. The Romans liked to honour their dead by visiting their graves and leaving gifts to help them in the afterlife.

Don't wave that dirty strigil at me or I'll put you in the mausoleum!

Yesterday we went to the cemetery to visit the grave of my uncle, Justinius, who was recently buried there in one of the mausolea.

We all took gifts for Uncle Justinius. Mine was an oil lamp, which Father said would help light the way for Uncle Justinius in the afterlife. I made the lamp with our local potter, who is friends with Father. It didn't look quite as good as the oil lamps sold at market but I was pleased with it.

After presenting our gifts, we ate our picnic lunch at the cemetery. It was a happy occasion.

Today, I went to the bathhouse. I liked having my back scraped with a strigil – a tool that gets rid of oil and dead skin. But the best bit was the plunge pool. It's freezing cold so you have to dip in and out very quickly!

This horse-shaped Roman brooch was discovered with the help of a metal detector in Derby in 2007.

Roman coins show the ruling emperor. This helps historians to work out dates.

How do we know?

What we know about Roman life in Derbyshire comes from the objects they lost or left behind – the remains of pots, tools and armour, lead ingots, offerings left in graves and sometimes jewellery.

The best Roman finds are from the Little Chester area of Derby where, in 1978, a Roman cemetery was found beneath what is now Derby Racecourse. It was a walled cemetery and held skeletons of civilians and soldiers. Two children's skeletons were found with objects including bronze bangles and a ring. Other graves contained the metal hobnails of boots, bits of armour and an iron blade.

Lots of Roman artefacts are on display at Derby Museum, including a roof tile with a dog's paw print in it and a jug spout shaped like a duck.

You can still see the remains of many Roman forts in Derbyshire.

CELT 500 BC	ROMAN AD 43–410	ANGLO-SAXON AD 450–1066	VIKING AD 865–1066	MEDIEV TIMES 1066–14

New Invaders

Annis and her family are working hard to build their new settlement in the Midlands. There is plenty of wood and water and the natives keep their distance. There are hills and a long, straight road nearby that traders pass along. There are also plenty of sheep, and the river for fishing. Annis thinks they will be happy here.

The Saxons are Here!

After the Romans left Britain in AD 410, other invaders began to arrive. They were the Angles and Saxons who crossed the North Sea from northern Europe. The newcomers settled here and gave their name to the country: Angle-land. Over time, this name became 'England'. English became an official language, alongside Latin, though most people could not read or write.

The Anglo-Saxons built a settlement less than 2 kilometres away from the old Roman 'vicus' in Derby. Their settlement was called Northworthy. There was cleared land for farming and plentiful natural resources, including wood, water and clay. At this time, Derbyshire was part of Mercia – an Anglo-Saxon region in the Midlands. For a long time, Repton was the capital of Mercia.

This Anglo-Saxon warrior's helmet was found in Monyash. It's on display at Weston Park Museum, Sheffield.

New Changes

Many Anglo-Saxons became Christians and, when Alfred became King of Wessex in AD 871, he made Christianity the official religion for England. Highly skilled Saxon craftworkers built impressive churches and carved amazing stone crosses. In the 8th century, a man called Alkmund gained a reputation for being charitable to the poor in Derby and, after his death in AD 800, he was made a saint. Today St Alkmund is the patron saint of Derby.

SPOT THIS!

St Alkmund's sarcophagus – a decorated stone coffin – can be seen in Derby Museum.

FUN FACT

The 'well' in Bakewell and Bradwell comes from the Old English word 'waella', meaning a spring.

The Anglo-Saxon Chronicle is a record of events in Saxon England. It was handwritten by monks.

How do we know?

Derbyshire's Anglo-Saxon treasures include the crypt under St Wystan's church at Repton, the warrior's helmet found at Benty Grange Farm in Monyash, a carved stone coffin lid now displayed at St Mary's Church in Wirksworth, and St Alkmund's sarcophagus.

Manuscripts decorated by hand by Saxon monks show how people dressed at that time. Formal wear for a Saxon lady was usually a long, plain shift dress with an over-tunic that was held in place by a pair of brooches. Grave goods for a rich Saxon lady have been excavated in Derby and are now on display in Derby Museum.

Vikings!

Rheda waits by the river, ready to hear the splash of the oars that means her father is coming home at last. Instead, she sees a great fleet of ships coming upstream. As they get closer, Rheda hears the deep grunt of the oarsmen. She knows something is wrong. As the first ship sails by, Rheda hears a shout and then she realizes. They are Vikings!

Move out of my way, Anglo-Saxon swine! We're in charge now!

The Vikings

Under the Anglo-Saxons, England had been divided into seven kingdoms. Derby was in the kingdom of Mercia, with Repton as its capital. But when the Vikings arrived from Denmark, they threatened to destroy the Saxon kingdoms.

King Alfred finally made peace with the Vikings, and England was divided into two halves. The south was controlled by the Saxons, while the north and the east, including Derbyshire, was ruled by the Vikings. They used Viking law – Danelaw – to control the people. The Vikings gave Derby its name, using two Norse words: 'der', meaning deer, and 'by', meaning settlement. With these words combined, Derby's name means 'a village where deer are found'.

...AD 874 VIKINGS INVADE REPTON AND DRIVE AWAY SAXON KING BURHRED...

Viking helmets did not have horns. Horned helmets risked injury to warriors on the same side.

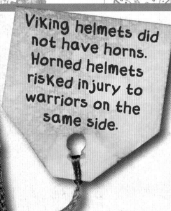

cool!

SPOT THIS!

Street names ending in 'gate' often come from the Viking word 'gata', meaning road. This one is in Chesterfield.

STEEPLEGATE

Derby was only a village in Viking times.

How do we know?

We can read about the Viking invasion of Repton in the Anglo-Saxon Chronicle. The record for AD 874 says: "This year went the army (the Vikings) from Lindsey to Repton, and there took up their winter-quarters, and drove the (Saxon) king, Burhred, over the sea, when he had reigned about two and twenty winters, and subdued all that land."

We also know that an important Viking leader died at Repton and was buried, with many Viking soldiers, in a single mass grave. This grave has been excavated and you can see the finds, such as the leader's sword and jewellery, in Derby Museum.

You can also see what a Viking warrior may have looked like! The head of a Viking, reconstructed from a skull found at Repton, was used in a television programme called 'Blood of the Vikings' and is also on display in the museum.

Building a Castle

The Norman baron is barking his orders again. Edwulf stands with his hands on his hips, angrily staring down at the baron. Why should he help to build a new home for this awful man? Edwulf and his family had been perfectly happy here before the Normans arrived. Now they are making all the local men build this new motte and bailey castle, with a wooden tower on the top. Edwulf takes a deep breath and gets back to work. If he got into trouble this baron could make life very difficult for his family.

Wait for me, King William! I'll help you control those northern rebels!

William Conquers All

In 1066, new invaders arrived. They were the Normans from Normandy in France. Their leader, William, defeated the Saxon King Harold at the Battle of Hastings, and became the new king of England. He was King William I, known as William the Conqueror.

In Derbyshire, the Normans took over the large Saxon estates owned by Edward the Confessor, then built strong castles. William de Peveril built his castle in the High Peak, overlooking the Peak Cavern. The Normans also turned quite a lot of Derbyshire into private hunting grounds. In 1086, King William sent his men all around the country to make a note of all the land, houses and animals that people owned. This information was recorded in the Domesday Book. Derbyshire had grand estates, with forests, fisheries, mills and farms.

Wonderful Wool

Medieval Derbyshire had a thriving wool trade. From the busy sheep farms, fleeces and yarn were taken to be sold at the many markets, as well as woollen cloth. In 1154, the king himself, Henry II, issued a royal charter granting Derby official permission to hold its market. There were many other skilled craftworkers and traders who sold goods there, including brewers, saddlers and blacksmiths.

SPOT THIS!

Some parts of Peveril Castle are from medieval times. Can you spot the Norman keep?

Derbyshire was beginning to grow in medieval times, thanks to the wool trade.

FUN FACT

Peak Cavern near Peveril Castle is also known as the Devil's Arse because of the rude noises that can be heard inside the cave!

How do we know?

The Domesday Book gives us a detailed record of Norman estates. As well as Peveril Castle at Castleton, we can see the remains of Norman castles at Horsley, Morley and Duffield.

In the 13th century, a monk of Dunstable wrote in his Chronicle that Derby wool was sold to foreign merchants as far away as Italy and Germany. A street in medieval Derby was named Full Street, where fullers turned wool into thick cloth.

CELT
500 BC

ROMAN
AD 43–410

ANGLO-
SAXON
AD 450–
1066

VIKING
AD 865–
1066

MEDIEVAL
TIMES
1066–1485

A Secret Plot

A Derbyshire gentleman, Sir Anthony Babington, is writing to Mary, Queen of Scots. His letter is in secret code. Sir Anthony is a Catholic and plans to assassinate Mary's cousin, Queen Elizabeth I. He knows this plot will endanger his own life but he has to try. Sir Anthony's groom is looking very worried. If he gets caught delivering the letter, he will be in serious trouble.

Treason!

Under Queen Elizabeth I, England was a Protestant country where Catholics could be put to death. Elizabeth's right to be queen was questioned by her Catholic cousin, Mary, Queen of Scots. So Elizabeth had Mary imprisoned for many years in country houses, including the newly-built Chatsworth House, Wingfield Manor and what is now the Old Hall Hotel in Buxton.

Sir Anthony Babington was a Catholic gentleman who came from a wealthy Derbyshire family. He hatched a plot to rescue Mary and assassinate Queen Elizabeth. But Sir Anthony's letter was discovered. He was executed for treason in 1586 and Mary was executed the following year.

FUN FACT

Chatsworth was built for a rich lady called Elizabeth, Countess of Shrewsbury. Her initials 'E.S.' can be found all over the house.

Civil War

In 1642, civil war broke out between supporters of Parliament and the Royalists, who supported the king. Sir John Gell of Wirksworth was a loyal tax gatherer for King Charles. But when war broke out, he changed sides and Derby became a Parliamentarian stronghold. There were several skirmishes between Royalists and Parliamentarians during the Civil War. The Parliamentarians eventually won and, in 1649, King Charles I was executed. For the next ten years, the country was ruled by a commoner, Oliver Cromwell.

TUDOR
1485–1603

STUART
1603–1714

GEORGIAN
1714–1837

VICTORIAN
1837–1901

MODERN TIMES
1901–NOW

A Brave Village

The Great Plague came to the village of Eyam in 1665. The vicar, William Mompesson, asked the villagers not to leave, in order to protect others. This is known as a quarantine. To avoid human contact, food and medicines were left outside the village at collection points such as Mompesson's well. Most of the villagers died but this brave action prevented further outbreaks in the surrounding area, saving hundreds of lives.

SPOT THIS!

Can you spot Mompesson's well, where supplies were left for the villagers of Eyam in 1665?

← Revolution House

Another Plot

In 1688, three noblemen plotted to depose the last Stuart king, James II. One of these men was the 4th Earl of Devonshire, from Chatsworth. The men invited the Dutch king, William of Orange, to take the throne. Their plot succeeded and became known as the 'Glorious Revolution'. The house where they met on Whittington Moor, just outside Chesterfield, is called Revolution House.

> With religious disputes and civil war, Derbyshire was an unsettled place to live in Tudor and Stuart times.

How do we know?

At St Werburgh's Church you can still see marks on the outer walls made by musket balls during the Civil War. Proof of the plague is found in the graves of the villagers who died in Eyam. You can also stand in the dell where Mompesson spoke to villagers about the quarantine.

Stagecoach

Sarah can't wait to get out of the stagecoach. She has been travelling for three days, bumping about in the coach with only the bleak Derbyshire moors outside the windows. She is looking forward to bathing in the spa at Buxton before calling on friends at the Assembly Rooms. There will be no dancing for Sarah, though. She's exhausted!

Leisure and Tourism

In the late 1700s, the roads across Derbyshire's moors were improved to help the many travellers who came by stagecoach to visit the new spas and public bathhouses in Buxton and Matlock. There were many coaching inns too. Both horses and passengers needed places to stop, where they could refresh themselves.

Travellers enjoyed the dramatic moors, hills and caves, and the new spa towns of Buxton and Matlock Bath. Both towns had natural water supplies, containing mineral salts, which were reputed to be good for you. They bathed in the bathhouses, drank the water at the Pump Rooms and socialized at the Assembly Rooms, where you could dance, chat or play cards with your friends.

The Bull i' the Thorn pub near Ashbourne was once a popular stop for stagecoaches.

...1714 GEORGE I BECOMES KING...1722 NEW SILK MILL BUILT IN DERBY...

A Bonnie Prince

Charles Edward Stuart was the grandson of James II, who had been removed from the throne during the Glorious Revolution. As heir to the Stuart throne, Charles was very angry about this. In 1745, Charles raised an army to take back the throne from King George II. The prince – nicknamed Bonnie Prince Charlie – marched his troops from Scotland towards London to fight the king. But when Charles reached Derby, he got word that the king's forces were much greater than expected. On the advice of his generals, Charles decided to turn back. King George II remained safely on the throne.

SPOT THIS!

Have you seen this statue of Bonnie Prince Charlie on Cathedral Green in Derby?

At Derby Museum there's a re-creation of the room in Exeter House where the prince made his decision to retreat.

WOW!

Great George

George Sorocold invented the Derby Water Supply. It was the first ever piped water supply and was soon copied all over the country. Sorocold also designed a silk mill in Derby, built in 1722. The story goes that he took a secret trip to Italy, where there was a thriving silk industry, and copied their ideas. When the mill was finished there were 10,000 spindles, all driven by a single water wheel. This was the country's first water-powered silk mill, putting Derby at the heart of the Industrial Revolution.

FUN FACT

George Sorocold died soon after his silk mill opened. Some say he was killed by an Italian assassin, having copied his design from Italy!

CELT 500 BC	ROMAN AD 43–410	ANGLO-SAXON AD 450–1066	VIKING AD 865–1066	MEDIEVAL TIMES 1066–1485

In the imaginary account on the right, a young boy tells us about his visit to a new mill in Cromford.

New mills were built all over Derbyshire, including this one: Arkwright's mill at Cromford.

The new mill looks wonderful, especially at night, when all the windows are ablaze with candles. It seems to have come from some great city to settle with us here in Cromford.

My brother is wrong to say that mill work is not for us. He works on the farm, like our father and grandfather. But I want to work with the big new machines in the mills. They spin a hundred times faster than an old spinning mule!

Tonight I shall go to the mill and ask for work. I shall be the best worker there and I will make Father proud of me.

Derwent Valley

Richard Arkwright

Another industrial pioneer, Richard Arkwright, set up a cotton spinning mill in Cromford in 1771. He had perfected a new spinning machine called a 'water frame', and used water from the River Derwent and other streams to power two huge water wheels. Mills were soon built along a 24-kilometre stretch of the Derwent. Arkwright built a whole new community of workers in Cromford and became known as the 'Father of the Factory System'.

China Works

Derbyshire became famous for its high-quality porcelain in the 18th century. William Pegg was 10 years old when he started work in a pottery. By the age of 15, he had taught himself to paint exquisite flowers on fine porcelain. Aged 21, he joined the Derby Porcelain works, now known as Royal Crown Derby. Later in life, William became a Quaker and decided that painting flowers was frivolous, so he gave it up.

The Derby Porcelain works, now known as Royal Crown Derby, made these figurines in about 1765.

Derby became famous for making some of the finest porcelain in the world.

How do we know?

Derbyshire was at the heart of the Industrial Revolution. It was home to many new inventions and the first ever factories.

Many of the mills, such as the one in Cromford, still exist today. But how do we know about the people who worked there? A boy called William Hutton was seven years old when he went to work at the Derby Silk Mill. He later wrote a book about his experiences. This anecdote describes Hutton's panic when he thinks he has overslept on a snowy morning in 1731: "I did not awake the next morning, till daylight seemed to appear. I rose in tears, for fear of punishment, and went to my father's bedside, to ask the time. He believed six; I darted out in agonies, and from the bottom of Full Street, to the top of Silk Mill Lane, not 200 yards, I fell nine times! Observing no lights in the mill, I knew it was an early hour, and the reflection of the snow had deceived me. Returning, the town clock struck two."

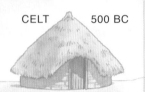

A Day Out

Amelia and her parents watch nervously as the iron monster emerges from a huge cloud of steam. It is the first locomotive they have ever seen. Amelia's Mama is terrified and thinks she will never ride on one, but Amelia is buzzing with excitement. Papa says Amelia is allowed to write to her cousin, Belinda, to invite her on a railway excursion to Matlock Bath. Amelia can't wait!

cool!

Great George!

The great engineer, George Stephenson, settled in Derbyshire in later life. Along with his son, Robert, George invented the early steam locomotive. At the time, people thought his steam engines were a very strange idea. Surely a team of strong men or horses was good enough to haul heavy wagons? The power of steam had been used before, to clear water from the mines, but now the Stephensons used it on 'railways' to link mines, quarries and ports with the busy factories.

In the 1840s, railway workshops were built near the railway station in Derby, providing engineers to build more locomotives. This provided jobs for local people for many years.

FUN FACT
Railway tracks had to be kept flat. Uphill routes would slow down the locomotives or even stop them altogether!

The 'Rocket' was invented by George and Robert Stephenson.

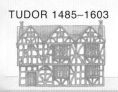

Railway Fever

Moving materials by railway proved faster and cheaper and soon the railways spread out all over the country, carrying goods by the shortest route possible. Then people wanted to travel by train too. In 1836, construction began on George Stephenson's North Midland Railway. Stephenson supervised the laying of a network of passenger railways that would take travellers from Derby as far as London, Scotland and the West Country. Meanwhile, a man called Thomas Cook, who was born in Melbourne in Derbyshire, arranged the first ever railway excursions.

SPOT THIS!

A stone in Holy Trinity Church, Chesterfield, marks the grave of George Stephenson.

New Problems

The new factories brought so many workers that towns soon became overcrowded. Large families had to live crammed together in back-to-back houses. With unhealthy water supplies and sewers, the poor faced sickness and death. More children under the age of five died than survived. Typhoid, spread by flies and poor hygiene, was a very common disease.

The Lady with the Lamp

William Nightingale was a Derbyshire gentleman with a family home in the village of Lea. His daughter, Florence, became a nurse. In 1854, Florence travelled to the Crimean War, to see how she could help the wounded soldiers. The soldiers called her 'The Lady with the Lamp' because she visited the wards at night, lighting her way with a lantern. Afterwards, Florence Nightingale laid down the rules for modern nursing and became perhaps the most famous nurse of all time.

Florence Nightingale advised on this statue on London Road, Derby, from the comfort of her bedroom!

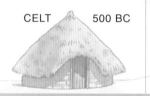
CELT   500 BC

ROMAN AD 43–410

ANGLO-SAXON AD 450–1066

VIKING AD 865–1066

MEDIEVAL TIMES
1066–1485

Having been granted permission by her father, Amelia is writing to her cousin, inviting her to Matlock Bath. This is an imaginary account.

I'm so excited about travelling on a locomotive! I do hope Cousin Belinda accepts my invitation.

11th May, 1840

Dear Cousin Belinda,

Are you seated comfortably to receive this exciting news? Papa has agreed to take us on the railway! You are cordially invited to join us for a day's excursion to the spa town of Matlock Bath, and we shall go by train to Ambergate and thereafter by carriage.

You must bring a blanket and a cushion, for Papa says the train will be very cold and the carriage very bouncy, especially if the horses are fresh.

Mama prays that the idea will fall through. She is fearful of the locomotive. Papa took us to the station to view it arriving. It is an iron monster, breathing fire and steam! Please write back soon and accept.

Yours, in anticipation and
with great affection,
Amelia

Thousands of Victorian day trippers visited the thermal waters in Matlock Bath. Today the baths are part of an aquarium.

FUN FACT
Bones from a hippopotamus, elephant and rhinoceros were dug up in Derby in Victorian times. They are about 120,000 years old!

Stephenson built the Anker Viaduct to carry the railway from Birmingham into Derby.

How do we know?

A report about the Derby area in 1837 tells us how the poor lived: "Many families are living in houses... unhealthy and over-crowded...during the whole of last summer a slow typhoid fever prevailed... throughout the winter a family of five children and mother and father nightly sleep in one stifling room."

A newspaper report from 1849 gives another account: "There are about 35 silk manufactories engaged in the various branches of the trade in Derby... about 5,000 people find employment. Refuse accumulates in house drains to a great extent; there are no local regulations for systematic drainage."

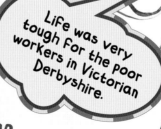

Life was very tough for the poor workers in Victorian Derbyshire.

23

 CELT
500 BC

 ROMAN
AD 43–410

 ANGLO-
SAXON
AD 450–
1066

 VIKING
AD 865–
1066

 MEDIEVAL
TIMES
1066–148

The Blitz!

It is dark and raining hard. Annie wants to go back to the house to fetch her pet hamster but her mum won't let her. Biting her lip, Annie reluctantly follows her sister into the air-raid shelter. She tries to put on her gas mask but the glass in front of her eyes keeps misting up. Then they hear a long, shrieking whistle. A bomb! The whistle stops and a few moments later there is a terrific blast. The whole garden seems to shake around them.

RAF Spitfire Fighter planes used during World War Two were powered by Rolls-Royce Merlin engines.

World War Two

During World War Two, Derby was a major target for enemy bombs, especially the engineering works at Rolls Royce and the locomotive works. The iron works at Stanton were a target too, as well as numerous munitions factories.

While many Derbyshire men went off to fight, everyone back at home had to carry identity cards and gas masks, in case of a deadly gas attack. People were issued with ration books filled with tokens to buy food. This ensured that there was enough food to share around. Most homes also had their own air-raid shelter. This might have been a Morrison shelter – a sort of cage with wire mesh sides that could also be used as a table – or an Anderson shelter, which was built outdoors.

Rolls Royce

Henry Royce and Charles Rolls were successful car manufacturers. Their 1907 Silver Ghost was hailed as the 'best car in the world'! During World War One, Rolls and Royce began making aero engines for fighter planes. Royce designed the Merlin engine in 1935 which went on to power the RAF Hurricanes, Spitfires and Lancaster bombers of World War Two.

SPOT THIS!

There are war memorials in almost every town and village in Derbyshire. This one is in Derby.

1939 – 1945

BURTON J.W.   SCOTT C.
COOK F.   SMITH A.
GEE J.   SMITH R.
HALES B.   STANNARD H.
HATTON J.W.   STIRK K.
HAYWOOD J.S.   TAVERNER F.T.
HINDLE J.W.   TREECE G.A.
KELLETT H.   TURNER C.
MILLER J.I.   WALKER C.
MOORE C.   WHITTINGHAM S
SALT F.A.   WOODWARD R.
LOWREY R.W.   FODWILL C.

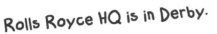
Rolls Royce HQ is in Derby.

The Bouncing Bomb

Have you ever skipped stones on a pond? A man called Sir Barnes Wallis, who was born in Ripley, used this idea to invent his 'Bouncing Bomb'. During World War Two, bombs were dropped on to the surface of German reservoirs, where they bounced along until they hit the dam walls that held back thousands of tons of water. When the dams burst, the German electricity supply was damaged and some armaments factories were completely flooded.

In 1943, the pilots of 617 Squadron, known as the Dambusters, practised for their difficult mission on the three dams of Derwent Dale: Howden, Derwent and Ladybower.

Peak District

As people began to have more leisure time, walking across the moors became a favourite pastime. But the ramblers were trespassing on the grouse moors of wealthy landowners and sometimes got into trouble. Finally, in 1949, a law was passed allowing free roaming rights on the moors and, in 1951, the very first UK National Park was created in the Peak District. Although people do have a 'right to roam' there are some rules about things like remembering to close gates and not dropping litter.

While enjoying a walk in the Peak District, look out for the millstones which mark its boundaries.

...1939–1945 WORLD WAR TWO...1943 DAMBUSTERS PRACTISE IN DERBYSHIRE...

25

CELT
500 BC

ROMAN
AD 43–410

ANGLO-
SAXON
AD 450–
1066

VIKING
AD 865–
1066

MEDIEVAL
TIMES
1066–1485

In this imaginary account, two boys called Jim and John are spying on the Dambuster planes as they make their practice runs at Ladybower Reservoir.

When I grow up, I want to be a Dambuster!

It was quite scary hiding in the bushes while guards patrolled the footpath behind us. John was the first to see the plane.

"See it?" he said excitedly. "It's coming!"

My stomach lurched like a trapped rabbit.

"It's too low!" I said.

"No," said John. "Watch." And we both stuck out our heads to witness the most amazing thing I've ever seen. The plane, flying so low I could see the pilot's face, dropped its load, then straightaway pulled upwards, its engines screaming.

Neither of us moved. We couldn't speak. The 'bomb' – not a real bomb, of course, as this was only a practice – skipped across the water like a bird: five, six, seven times. Then it sank, with only a few ripples to show where it had been.

"Did you see that?" John breathed.

"I did! I did!" I whispered.

The Dambusters used bags of flour as bombs in their practice runs at Ladybower.

26

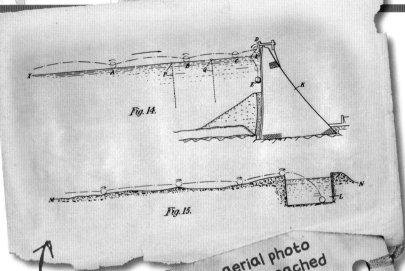

Sir Barnes Wallis drew this plan for the 'Bouncing Bomb'.

This aerial photo shows the breached Möhne Dam in Germany after the 'Dambusters' attack.

How do we know?

In 2009, a heritage plaque in honour of Sir Barnes Wallis was erected in Ripley. It describes him as "Designer of airships, aeroplanes, the 'Bouncing Bomb' and swing-wing aircraft". At Derwent Dam you can see a memorial to the 617 Dambuster Squadron.

Meanwhile, Rolls Royce engines can be found powering half of all the passenger jets in the world!

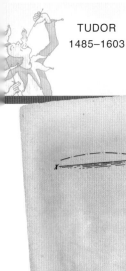

Do you know the Dambusters theme tune?

This Rolls Royce Trent 900 jet engine is part of an Airbus A380 on display at an air show.

Today and Tomorrow

Derbyshire's history can be discovered in lots of ways. The important thing to remember is that it is about the people who lived through difficult or exciting or dangerous times. What else is Derbyshire known for?

⬆ Chatsworth House is one of the most popular stately homes in Britain. Do you think it will still be standing in another 500 years?

Centuries of coal mining came to an end in the 1980s, when most pits were closed. Look out for the winding wheels set up as memorials in Derbyshire. ➡

⬆ Millstones in the Peak District are a reminder of Derbyshire's industrial heritage. Will they remain there for future generations?

SPOT THIS!

Brian Clough led Derby County FC into the semi-finals of the European Cup in 1973.

⬆ The Quad is an arts centre in Derby, completed in 2008. Its design was quite controversial at first. What do you think? Do you like it?

The villages of the White Peak show their well dressings every year to say thank you for the water. Can you think of any other Derbyshire traditions? ➡

You should feel proud to be from Derbyshire.

FUN FACT
Dame Ellen MacArthur is a long-distance yachtswoman from Matlock. In 2005, she broke the world record for sailing solo around the world.

How will they know?

Will Derbyshire always look like it does today? How will future generations know about our Derbyshire? Modern technology ensures that millions of first-hand accounts, photographs, pieces of art and music, and thoughts of everyday life will give people in the future a strong understanding of what Derbyshire is like for us, now.

Glossary

AD – a short way to write Anno Domini, which is Latin and means 'in the year of Our Lord', i.e. after the birth of Christ.

Air raid – an attack during World War Two when German planes dropped bombs on Britain. Air-raid sirens sounded to warn people to hide in their nearest air-raid shelter.

Armaments – weapons and vehicles used for war.

Artefact – an object, often an archaeological one.

Assassin – a murderer, especially someone who kills a person of importance.

Blitz – when Germans bombed towns during World War Two, it was called the Blitz.

Catholic or **Roman Catholic** – a member of the Christian religion that considers the Pope its head.

Cemetery – ground set aside for the dead to be buried in.

Charter – written permission to do something. A royal charter means the king or queen has given permission.

Christian – one who believes Jesus Christ is the son of God and follows his teachings.

Christianity – the name of the religion whose followers believe Jesus Christ is the son of God.

Civil war – a war where people in the same country fight each other.

Crypt – an underground room, often in a castle or church, used as a chapel or for burial.

Depose – to use force to take someone out of a position of power or authority.

Domesday Book – a record of who owned property, land and animals in England in 1086.

Excavate – to dig up buried objects in order to find out about the past.

Execute – to kill a person who has been sentenced to death.

Fort or **fortress** – a large, strong building offering military support and protection.

Gas mask – used in World War Two, this mask prevented you from breathing poisonous gas.

Ingot – a block of metal.

Latin – the language of ancient Rome.

Mausoleum – a very big tomb, usually for someone important.

Parliamentarian – anyone who fought on the side of Oliver Cromwell and Parliament in the English Civil War. Also known as a Roundhead.

Port – a place next to land where the water is deep enough for ships to stop and stay.

Protestant – a member of the Christian religion that considers the king or queen of England to be the head of its church.

Quaker – a group of Christians, also known as the Society of Friends.

Quarantine – to keep people or animals apart from others, to avoid spreading a contagious disease.

Quarry – a large area of land where stone is dug or blasted out of the ground.

Ration book – issued during World War Two, a ration book contained tokens which you exchanged for food.

Royalist – anyone who fought on the side of King Charles I in the English Civil War. Also known as a Cavalier.

Treason – the action of betraying someone or something, such as your country or monarch.

Index

Acknowledgements

The author would like to thank the following people for their generous help:
Joan D'Arcy of the Derby Local History Group, for help with the Roman history of Derby;
the Revd David J. Horsfall, Rector of Holy Trinity Church in Chesterfield, for information about George Stephenson;
and the staff of Matlock Library, the Local Studies Library and the Derbyshire Local Records Office.

The publishers would like to thank the following people
and organizations for their permission to reproduce material:
Front cover: Duncan Payne/Shutterstock; back cover: Bill Wright/Flickr; p1: Jon Bennett/Wikipedia; p7: image provided courtesy of the Portable Antiquities Scheme, Fishbourne Roman Palace, Chichester; p8: Nathandbeal/Wikipedia; p9: Eamon Curry/Flickr; p11: York Archaeological Trust, www.jorvik-viking-centre.co.uk; p13: John Stanbridge/Flickr; p15: Sion Harrison and Jill Sargent/Flickr, Jon Bennett/Wikipedia; p16: Christopher Shaw/Flickr; p17: George Cole/Flickr, Richard Miller/Flickr; p18: Steve Trice/Flickr; p19: Royal Crown Derby Museum; p21: Russ Hamer/Wikipedia; p22: Globuss Images/Alamy; p23: Bill Wright/Flickr; p24: Paul Drabot/Shutterstock; p25: Ricardo Demurez/Alamy; p26: Robin Navamanie/Flickr; p27: Mary Evans/The National Archives, Illustrated London News Ltd/Mary Evans, Antony Nettle/Alamy; p28: Dave Younce/Flickr, Duncan Harris/Flickr, Paul Newcombe/Flickr, Russ Hamer/Flickr, LauraKidd/Amplified2010/Wikipedia; p29: www.iknow-peakdistrict.co.uk, Whaley Tim/Wikipedia.

Written by Pauline Chandler
Educational consultant: Neil Thompson
Designed by Sarah Allen
Edited by Gemma Cary

Illustrated by Kate Davies, Dynamo Ltd, Virginia Gray,
Peter Kent, John MacGregor, Leighton Noyes and Tim Sutcliffe.
Additional photographs by Pauline Chandler

First published by HOMETOWN WORLD in 2012
Hometown World Ltd
7 Northumberland Buildings
Bath BA1 2JB

www.hometownworld.co.uk

ISBN 978-1-84993-244-8

CELT
500 BC

ROMAN
AD 43–410

ANGLO-SAXON
AD 450–1066

VIKING
AD 865–1066

MEDIEVAL TIMES
1066–1485